Wishing Tree

Also by Geoff Graetz and published by Ginninderra Press
Magical Sputnik
Music of Our Sphere (Pocket Poets)

Geoff Graetz

Wishing Tree

Wishing Tree
ISBN 978 1 76109 444 6
Copyright © Geoff Graetz 2022

First published 2022 by
Ginninderra Press
PO Box 3461 Port Adelaide 5015
www.ginninderrapress.com.au

Contents

Foreword	7
Places	
Old Wisanger School	11
New Zealand Suite	12
Along the Road to Tibooburra	17
Port Elliot 2020	19
River Stroll	20
Wagtail's Woe	21
Garden of Earthly Delights	22
Koori Country	23
People and Feelings	
Embarrassed	27
Fame	28
Anxious Thoughts	29
Listen Long	30
Upward Stride	31
You Need a Plan	32
Riding in Lycra	33
Flashes of Colour	34
In Friendship's Bond	35
Together Again	36
Memories	
Favourite Game	39
Gems From Grandma's Album	40
My Shiny Kitbag	41
Lashing Rain	42
Girl In Pink Tutu	43
Evacuate	44

Attitudes and Concerns

Rolling Money	47
Magnetic Dream	48
Wind in Our Hair	49
Cumulus Gold	50
Child Saplings	51
Nature's Face	52
Unless We Listen	53

Affairs of the World

Defiance	57
Lion Pride	58
Collars Blue and White	60
Lyndoch, Sunday Afternoon	61
Pandemic haiku	62
Junkyard Dog	63
Blinding Flash	64
Wishing Tree	65
Partners Light Our Sphere	67

Time to Smile

Argy-bargy	71
T-Bone	72
Brain Games	73
Mathematics acrostic	74
Belly Laugh	75
Bully Boy	76
Winston's Words of Wisdom	77

Previously Published	78
About the Author	79

Foreword

I am pleased to present this collection of poems combining observation, social comment and a touch of whimsy.

My thanks go to the members of my local writing group, Chapter and Verse, for the stimulus they have provided for my writing, including workshops presented by gifted writers which have also expanded my horizons.

I also wish to thank Vivian Garner and Jude Aquilina for their valuable editing of my work. In addition, my wife Ruth has made many helpful suggestions.

Thank you also to Stephen Matthews for his help in publishing this book.

Places

Old Wisanger School

opened on Kangaroo Island as the Farmers' Assembly Room in 1864

I stood at the open gate
pictured farmers laying limestone
white, square and true
a place to talk of rain, of sowing and reaping.

Soon the children of Mary and Henry
arrived with friends for school
their teacher bringing water and coal
giving lessons in copperplate spelling

shaping nibs for ink-dipped pens
flexing the cane that gave a nasty sting.
One lady teacher carried her baby
over the hills from Emu Bay.

I saw children saluting the Union Jack
reading names from the map of the Empire.
Sometimes boys stayed home for harvest
helping Dad to reap the bearded grain.

Girls learnt embroidery art
stitching calico samplers in coloured thread.
Children free to roam the tree-fringed yard
and play their happy lunchtime games.

Too soon, some boys grew to wear khaki uniform
girls grew to wear white gowns and veils.

All their memories clear, written so well
indelible in life's exercise book.

New Zealand Suite

Christchurch
a city devastated by an earthquake in 2011

Christchurch is Totahi, place of the chief
now rising from grey rubble
accompanied by growl of machines
cheered by cheeky murals
one declaring, JELLY CITY.

The Avon flows, quietly sinuous
not far from chain fences and jack hammer staccato
and a mall has popped up, dressed in red
and yellow
beautified shipping containers
one filled with fashionable dresses.

Heritage masonry bolted and propped
stands defiantly
a shattered building fronted by a crane
declares SMASH PALACE
185 white chairs mutely speak
of the lives taken and remembered.

The cracked cathedral sits uneasily
its A-framed cardboard cousin
wears a carbonate roof halo
giving sanctuary within a city of building sites.

The city in the pangs of rebirth
its new buildings defying subterranean shivers
sporting colourful murals of hope
for a happier life.

Dunedin
the city centre has an octagonal park

Robbie Burns gazes over his octagon
while people sit and rest or hurry on.

Later we hear the piper's haggis tune
and Robbie's verse – the pudding rune.

Glasses raised, a toast is sipped
his verse from memory hasn't slipped.

We are piped to dining room
to feast on haggis – what a boon.

Coach Captain

Captain Ian whirls his coach through mountain ranges
while telling stories of friends and strangers.

Makes us rise early every day
and cheers us all along the way.

And when we start to squirm and hop
calmly announces *Comfort stop*.

Proudly rolls through his home town
his local knowledge knows no bounds.

Parks his coach under rocky peak
a photo stop with views to keep.

Drives us round some lakes serene
and Good Shepherd Church with inspiring scene.

At journey's end he's earned a cheer
and a gift with which to buy a beer.

Bull

We were on the road to Rotorua
when we entered the town of Bull.
I tell you it's a story so pure
the town hall was signed *Social-bull.*

If anyone went speeding through
the police station has a *Consta-bull.*
There may be bins red and blue
but yellow ones were labelled *Recycla-bull.*

If in this town I wanted to stay
the real estate agent has homes *Renta-bull.*
And when hunger comes my way
the café, of course, has food *Delecta-bull.*

If you think that from the truth I stray
Our coach load of tourists shouts, *It's no bull!*

Rotorua

Take me back to the lakes of Rotorua
where hills ring the town and geysers perform
but the breeze in the trees is not so pure
sulphur rises come dusk and dawn.

Tourist coaches discharge their folks
hoi polloi roam and wander
learn a lesson from White Island boats
where lava rolls and volcanoes thunder.

Here, fumaroles fume and rocks feel hot
where can all that heat be coming from?
Red-hot magma could be their lot
will lava rise to explode like a bomb?

Wellington

Wellingtonians know how to party
Saturday streets filled with stalls so crafty.

People in costume perform for the crowd
food stalls have many more standing around.

Bare-chested young men climb a harbour tower
somersaults into cold water show off their power.

We pause for an ice cream tasty and smooth
so many flavours, it's hard to choose.

The Beercycle starts out on its run
on board eight pedallers out to have fun.

We all drink responsibly they loudly chant
while pedalling along, drink beer as they rant.

Past Te Papa Tongawera, Museum of New Zealand
and ghosts of wharfies loading ships by hand.

Now it's a place on Saturday night
to have a good time, that's everyone's right.

New Zealand Haiku

mountain slopes swoop down
meets glittering sea
plunges into the depths

gentle ocean swell
rolls till a shudder from below
rears into a bad tsunami

placid ocean green
kayakers on Cathedral Cove
worship the stone arch

Along the Road to Tibooburra

Once some jolly tourists camped by a billabong
under the shade of a coolabah tree:
they sang as they watched and waited till their lunch was ready,
'You'll come a-waltzing matilda with me.'

> 'Waltzing matilda, waltzing matilda,
> You'll come a-waltzing matilda with me.'
> They sang as they watched and waited till their lunch was ready,
> 'You'll come a-waltzing matilda with me.'

Down came a heifer to drink at the billabong
up jumped the tourists and grabbed her with glee;
they sang as they put that heifer in their tucker bag,
'You'll come a-waltzing matilda with me.'

> 'Waltzing matilda, waltzing matilda,
> You'll come a-waltzing matilda with me.'
> They sang as they put that heifer in their tucker bag,
> 'You'll come a-waltzing matilda with me.'

Up drove the manager, riding in his four wheel drive,
up came policemen, one, two, three,
'Where's that little heifer you've got in your tucker bag?
You'll come a-waltzing matilda with me.'

> 'Waltzing matilda, waltzing matilda,
> You'll come a-waltzing matilda with me
> Where's that little heifer you've got in your tucker bag?
> You'll come a-waltzing matilda with me.'

Up jumped the tourist guide and sprang into a motorboat,
'You'll never catch me for spray,' said he.
And his voice may be heard as you walk along that billabong,
'You'll come a-waltzing matilda with me.'

    'Waltzing matilda, waltzing matilda,
    You'll come a-waltzing matilda with me.'
    And his voice may be heard as you walk along that billabong,
    'You'll come a-waltzing matilda with me.'

Port Elliot 2020

A stroll under Norfolk pines
brass memorials to fallen soldiers
twinkly blue ripples below on Horseshoe Bay
yellow machine shatters the peace
growling at surf clubrooms
giant claw ripping timber and steel

snarling
grabbing
swivelling

dropping entrails into wide mouthed trailer
orange hi-vis worker smiles
Yes, they're going to build a new one.

Sparkly waves gently break
a child climbs on nearby playground castle
ignoring the monster behind the fence.
Maybe she will swim as a Nipper in the new club.

River Stroll

I love to walk beside river gums
huge monuments Heysen loved to paint
more like living statues
home to laughing kookaburras
gracious giants of the Gawler River.

The King Tree, patriarchal personage
ancient ruler in its Wirrabara paddock
crowd of offspring spread around
viewed in awe by tourist troves
gasping at great sloping girth.

I feel calmed, walking in the shade
under great arms spreading overhead
hollows above for nesting cockatoos
Eucalyptus air wafting in the breeze
gives me peace among the rustling leaves.

Wagtail's Woe

Through the window glass
my eyes are drawn to a gnarled melaleuca
and a swooping wagtail
beak-snapping an ebony raven
a hundred times bigger.

Ducking the chattering beak
and desperate dives
giant white eyes swivel
to search the tangled branches.

Descending into the depths
the giant clambers up again
spotted egg in its beak.
Willy falls silent.

I want the sad silent mourners
to hatch other eggs
chicks to gobble insect dinners
and grow to dance and chatter.

I wonder at jungle law
long for a world in balance
between tiny flitting nations
and neighbours a hundred times bigger.

Garden of Earthly Delights

I do like to be in the garden
the dark, damp earth for me
it's a global layer, God-given
a gift of life for petunia and pea.

To cultivate, compost and rake
as I recall Dr Cooper's refrain
long ago, a remark he'd often make
anything that has lived can live again.

My fingers stretch to plant seedling and shrub
watering and watching them grow.
I look closely for aphid and grub
waiting for colourful fruit and flower show.

My leaf-mould mulch spread on the soil
a feast for worms both great and small.
making food for leaves is their daily toil
so that my trees grow straight and tall.

Natives like grevillea and tea tree
my special joy across the ground
a bonanza for honeyeater and bee
where scented pollen feasts abound.

Dr Wilfred Shewell-Cooper was a British organic gardener and pioneer of no-dig gardening.

Koori Country

on the land of the Jarwadjali; Gariwerd – the Grampians

I like it when I am free
and walking in the bush
to sound of wind in top of tree
far away from shove and push.

The ears of kangaroo
swivel at my sound
while screech of cockatoo
to me is music all around.

But if I were a first Australian
wallaby I'd hunt and track
before invasion first began
now lambs graze; too late to hand it back.

For Koori, this land is Country
my thoughts rush like water in the creek
no longer am I so carefree
they need this land to love and keep.

People and Feelings

Embarrassed

Entering the room
My face is red
Bowed by laughter
Adding to my gloom
Reeling as from a blow
Ready to hide
Agitated eyes
Seeking escape route
Salve for my brow
Errant thoughts bounce around
Desperate to dive for cover.

Fame

For some
the road winds slowly
ascending the foothills
to a money-clad mountain peak
and a hacienda mirrored in a glacial lake
until…the black curtain falls.

For others
a long sloping road
rising above startling ballyhoo
ascending to peaks of power
and an eyrie atop a gleaming tower
until…a rival's bid succeeds.

And for a few
a circling road
rising upward, stepping forward then sliding back
persisting to reach a snow-clad summit
admired by millions across the plains
forever etched…on history's page.

Anxious Thoughts

The dreaded words so softly spoken
Tests show a tumour, her heart is broken
daggers appear above her head
as if hanging by a thread.
Soon the surgeon's scalpel gently strokes
seeking not to deny her hopes.

    In times of trouble just like this
    anxious thoughts thread through the mind
    Life is short, they seem to say
    spiralling downwards into darkened space.

Now in recovery, her eyes slowly blink
nurses bustle, little time to think
until her surgeon's voice quietly sensitive
I'm glad to say it was a false positive.
Deep breaths, a tear or two

    her tensions ease from red to blue

    her life can follow the path she's chosen
beckoning her to a new horizon.

Listen Long

Nerves stretched like violin strings
shoulders drooping, head cast down
pursed lips, heavy eyes
hard the way from lows to highs.

Some friends we meet are full of talk
we hear of cruise to palm-clad isle
we nod and smile with cheery grin
while gloomy thoughts we hide within.

How much we need ears attuned
lips to ask, *How are you going?*
eyes to see our downcast look
and read our face just like a book.

with a look that says, *I understand*
to listen long without a pause
hear our heartfelt speech
a hug or handshake within reach.

Upward Stride

I gazed over titanium beach
the headland so far out of reach.
I ran along with springing stride
beside the sparkling, rippling tide.

A voice called me from on high
as dunes reached toward the sky
Run this way, it seemed to say
This is your path, come what may.

I turned, began to run upslope
my arms swinging with all good hope
my feet sank into grainy sand
how I needed a helping hand.

Rocket plants and spiky mounds
marked my straining muscle bounds
The voice said, 'You're at the crest.'
Life led me up, now time to rest.

Looking far across the bay
it was here I longed to stay.
The voice said, 'More peaks ahead.'
So down and up again I tread.

You Need a Plan

You need a plan
if you want to ride a bull
not a list on white paper
a string of dot points.

When you are bucked off
by a bad-tempered shorthorn
dumped in the dust
blue bruises rising…

you need a plan
a picture of your determined stare
to get back on again…

and ride the beast home.

Riding in Lycra

lyric for a song

Pedalling down the road
cars keep off a metre
carrying their load
then we're round the corner.

Derailleur gears so smooth
hills are not a worry
our legs run in a groove
until we reach the gully.

Lycra stripes outshining
all that four wheeled driving.

Country town's fine bakery
the place we like to rest
enjoying camaraderie
coffee and cake the best.

Now we ride homeward bound
vineyard green, blue range above
far behind, peaceful town
refreshed, the ride we love.

Lycra stripes outshining
all that four-wheeled driving.

Flashes of Colour

You and the black dog
behind locked door
until – exercise hour comes.

You walk the black dog
tail drooping
streets grey, lined with blank windows

cold breeze
charcoal clouds hang low
signals of rain.

Your eyes bleary, downcast
dragging black dog
you round a corner

spy some tiny treasures
pastel pink blossoms –
a pocket of magic.

Warmed by flashes of colour
you look around
the black dog has faded away…faded away.

In Friendship's Bond

In friendship's bond, the listening ear
the gentle nod helps face the lurking fear
concern written upon their faces
universal light across all human races
bringing a sense of cheer
    in friendship's bond.

Times when eyes glisten with a tear
coming at any time of year
hands across tables in quiet corner places
    in friendship's bond.

Where are friends of yesteryear?
Perhaps old pals are no longer here
yet their warmth lingers on in mem'ries traces
kindly eyes, one of many long-loved graces
words of comfort one longed to hear
    in friendship's bond.

Together Again

for Shirley and Milton, married 65 years

Night rain pattered on the roof
then after sunrise, climbing rose blessed
with a thousand rain drops
hanging like diamonds on leafy stems.

On one russet-edged leaf
a pair of sparkling droplets
slowly drifting down
the leafy valley
side by side
until they clung to the very edge.

Sun descended, and with a gentle flutter,
she quietly fell.
Shadows lengthened.
His grip trembling, until
he followed like a teardrop.

The two silently settled
into the welcoming earth
as one again.

Memories

Favourite Game

Players crouch, coiled – like springs
thump of fist on ball
parabola high over the net
pounded return
drops like a bomb.

Fists clenched, I dive
just in time
I send the ball upwards
our spiker's smash
rains fear on our opponents.

Desperate lunge sends ball high.
Eyes raised
we spring like gazelles
to strike a return.

Volleyball
my favourite game.

Gems From Grandma's Album

riverbank friends
a bride and groom
honeymoon stroll by the sea

folding camera in black and silver
steady hands
viewfinder squint

last frame captured
film rewound
so many precious gems

red glow of darkroom
developer dish rocking
soon negative faces appear
moments of time in reverse

images projected on paper
as light shines in the gloom
glossy sheets rocked and rinsed
black and white beauty left to dry

may these jewels of memory
survive the years
and children's children remember

My Shiny Kitbag

You wore my name in gold
painted by the local signwriter.
You carried my newly covered exercise books
as I lugged you aboard the yellow school bus.
Your gold letters matched my blazer's braid
as I wondered, *Who am I.*
What will high school be like?
We rode past my tree-lined one-teacher school
remembering happy schoolyard games.
I sat by myself, my friends on the train
sent to technical high by dictator parents.
You were my constant companion
as I took my place
in a green wooden classroom.
Gold letters, gold braid
would Gawler High be gold?
Looking back I say, *Yes*
after a string of years
twenty-four-carat gold.

Lashing Rain

May 1952, our poultry farm
rain lashed the chooks
wet feet in their yards
not laying well.

Winter, years passing
rubber-booted, I trod in mud
rain coat most days
centipede hiding under damp mat.

Navel oranges floating around trees
silty water from Gawler River
brought upriver farmers' fertiliser
later, juicy oranges abounded.

Winter 1956, rain cascading
mighty Murray flooded the plains
only roofs showing at Blanchetown.
Will those days ever return?

Girl In Pink Tutu

A little blonde girl
dances in pink tutu
for Mums and Dads
in bare Goodwood Hall.

In a line of lively friends
smiling as they sing
bouncing with the music
wide eyes form happy circles.

They bow to cheers from all
maybe the path to ballet school
or the stage of *Sound of Music*
for the girl in a pink tutu.

Evacuate

A continental hot breath
a car beeps past our house
EVACUATE.

A cloud of white smoke turning black
billows above western trees
wind relentless from the north.

Grabbing a bag, water bottle
with my neighbour I escape
community centre crowd swells.

Noisy chatter, stories told
dogs on leads, water bowls out
cats recline in cages.

Clocks tick, time slows
punctuated by cups of tea
yellow suited reporters appear.

My battery radio murmurs
of fires far and near
but when can we go home?
Gentler winds at sunset
Lucy's quiet word, *The road is open.*
Our house unscarred in green and gold.

Attitudes and Concerns

Rolling Money

Money is round and rolls away
falling into tills and pockets
until the bell tolls
warning of empty purse or wallet.

My plastic card is tapped too often
swiped over money-hungry machines
sweeping bank ledgers clean
and turning black numbers to red.

The banker wants a pound of flesh
interest makes red figures jump
feeble payments fitfully dance
no avenue to start afresh.

My brain needs abrushing clean
when storewide bargains shout and sing.
It must be time to clamp my card
before the tide of red rebounds.

Magnetic Dream

He sat abeam his trusty screen
as if held in a magnetic dream.
You have won ten thousand. To claim
send banking numbers, delight your brain.
Visions of coral beaches bade him reply
Don't let these hopes to me deny.

Rarely it comes and unforeseen
a gift in our hands with a golden sheen.
Who knows why these things come to us
when they do, we love to grasp in eager trust.

Came the day and hour to reckon
when palm treed islands to him would beckon.
Instead, his treasure vault lay cold and bare
miseries assaulted his head of greying hair.

Slowly dawns the cold light of day
when fear creeps across the hopeful face.
Magnetic dreams easily ensnare
so heed the sign, *Let the buyer beware.*

Wind in Our Hair

When the world looks dark
heavy weights pressing on shoulders
troubles rising like mountains
    everyone should fly a kite.

On the ribbon beach
salty breeze in our face
struggling to be free
    we could fly our kite.

Feel the playful tug
the joy of swooping thing
see the colours dancing
    as we fly our kite.

Spirits soaring on high
carry our thoughts skyward
hearts warmly glow
    as we fly a kite.

Wind in our hair
delightful joy of flight
raised up to a higher being
    to the heavens fly a kite.

Cumulus Gold

I am a cumulus queen
figures I see below
deep in grudge and groan
now they look up
gazing at my rising powers.

My rosy vapours
tumble ever higher
lit by golden glow.

Grey and gloom melt away
under my smile in flaming red.
The travellers now stepping out
transported up and beyond
led by my roseate smile.

Child Saplings

Grey-green seedlings
soon to be saplings
stretch ever skyward.
I wish I could give them
hope they will silently rise
full-limbed, broad in trunk
watered by winter river swirl
larrikin lorikeets feeding
on their red gum pollen
raucous kookaburras
laughing across golden heavens
crimson rosellas peering
from their high-rise hollows.
I also wish I could give
child saplings hope
to rise, heavenward
feeding, being fed
to stand, well-footed
firmly in flooding rain
knowing joy, like lorikeets
able to laugh with kookaburras
hands spread to the sky like leaves reaching for the sun.

Nature's Face

Coal-black smoke billows from chimneys
invisible fumes spouting from exhaust pipes.

Ash-grey cattle roam browning outback plains
hillsides carpeted with tree stumps.
Rivers brown in raging torrents.
Pacific blue tides swamp coral atolls.
Purple-grey in leaping anvil clouds
and stinging spray in cyclonic gales.
Orange in rolling, gritty dust.
White in creeping sand dunes
Nature's face inflamed and angry.

When will enough be enough
as young people take to the streets?
Will cool heads prevail
to ban the plunder of nature's treasures?

Unless We Listen

Words taste as sweet as honey
    the stringybark,
Take care of me, I make oxygen
    the dugong,
Keep my water pure for my calves
    the cassowary,
Protect my forests, I sow seeds.

People of hard foreheads and stubborn hearts
    close their ears
    burn oil, make money
    plastic scattered, we don't care
    chop down trees, mine coal.

A rainbow clad angel towers above
    right foot on the sea
    left foot on the land
speaking words of warning
    fire shall fall on the forests
    waters turn to blood
    plagues strike the earth.

Words sweet as honey turn sour in the gut
    unless we listen.

Affairs of the World

Defiance

Held tight in my phalanx
shield and baton ready
I face the city barricade.
Shouts echo from glass towers.

The chanting crowd carpets the boulevard
waving loud banners.
A bearded young man steps up
fist upraised, shouting defiance.

I hear the sergeant bark
He's the one, bring him in.
In vee formation we surge forward
truncheons flailing; we pin his arms

drag him, bruised, to our van
door slammed shut.
My private thoughts intrude
Is his courage greater than ours?

We are many, he is one.
Are others, like him, roving the streets?
My fleeting vision: our prisoner,
on a beribboned dais, orating as President.

Lion Pride

Boasting the glossy Lion badge
the hardy Holden
a wheeled way of life.

Blokes in their oily sheds
tamed noisy tappets
of the friendly FJ.

The Kingswood appeared
king of family cars
room for the bassinet in the back.

Next, the trendy Torana
the pride of long-haired youth
who prowled in their SLR.

The muscled Monaro
loud roar from its exhaust
paced hills and highways.

The compact Commodore
carried folks to work and beach
and won many a supercar race.

Cool and comfortable, the Caprice
basked in the boss's drive
or stood proudly beside many a cellar door.

As popular as the meat pie
(with sauce)
as far spread as the kangaroo.

From the big coat hanger
to outback waterhole
how the lion roared.

Collars Blue and White

Collars blue and white
factory's racket proud
flooded with fluoro light.

Designs boldly drawn
sleeves rolled up, ties askew
here great ideas are born.

White collars cannot give them birth
collars blue on machine shop floor
how much their skills are worth.

Top notch gifts of eye and hand
lathe and borer spin and cut
blue print and monitor often scanned.

On the line are engine parts well made
assembled, primed to roar into life
engineers need the skilful workers' trade.

Lyndoch, Sunday Afternoon

Sunny Sunday, village green
two bikers chatting
parents and two kids walking
one man on veranda opposite
throws a frisby for his dog
bakery and hotel closed
lonely car drones by
police car following.

All is eerily quiet
as we walk on lonely footpaths
past rose-hedged vineyard
along deserted streets.

Back home, we hear tourists
had passed through
virus-stricken.

No one told us
we enjoyed the red roses.

Pandemic haiku

stay arm's length apart
it's law carved on stone tablets
so easily broken

Meerkats standing tall
round eyes search for children's smiles
please open zoo gates

Sparrows perch on a sign
look down at empty main street
no people, no crumbs

Junkyard Dog

Junkyard Dog trotting
past ferro-red bodies
death valley of cars.
Maralinga Dog following
Aboriginal nomad family
past overturned Land Rovers
lying in plutonium dust.
Hairless Hiroshima Dog
skirting twisted steel skeletons
tail between its legs
too close to ground zero.
Space Dog, capsule bound
zooming around blue planet
through a cloud of a thousand dots
gleaming across ink-black dome.
Today, junk on collision course
send up a recycle skip
before it's too late.

Junk: 23,000 fragments over 100 millimetres in size, 500,000 less than 100 millimetres in low earth orbit speeding at up to 2,000 kilometres an hour (*National Geographic*, 2020)

Blinding Flash

A
blinding flash,
classroom in fiery flames.
One burned little boy dragged
from red hot ruins by a soldier
to the river doused in cool relief
hearing his name in the distance
cried, 'Daddy', tears streaming.
All around swirling black mist
Magenta fires raging
'Water!' blackened
victims called
helpers ran
bringing wet cloths
Hibakusha in many thousands.

A belly has opened,	Little Boy dropped
the first atomic bomb,	born from Enola Gay.
Little boys and girls,	Mums and Dads
all gone in a flash	of blinding light.
Hiroshima	Nineteen forty-five.

Hibakusha: the victims of Hiroshima and Nagasaki

Wishing Tree

A party at home
too many drinks
punches thrown
guests told *Get out.*

Partners yelling
hair-raising screams
then…silence…until
next day – red and blue lights flash.

Kirra's 105 bruises
an adult with *shaken baby syndrome*
her mother's embrace at hospital bed
brain death
four children motherless.

*

How much I'd like to see
in every town a wishing tree
where women bruised in hidden places
sadness writ upon their faces
come to tell their inmost fears
with Cinderella's silent tears.

Godmother of golden hair
descending from castle in the air
to outwit the ugly men
sending them to sit in inky den.

Bringing a coach of glassy hue
bound wherever love is true
a place that's always warm and snug
there to feel a kindly hug.

A wishing tree in every town
and godmother in her fairy gown.

Partners Light Our Sphere

Flaming sunset afar
beaten brassy sphere settling
beyond ragged row of pines
pairs of galahs gliding homeward.

Eastern magenta curtain
rises into velvet space
welcoming aureate sphere
riding majestically above town roofs.

East and West portray
two partners
linked in Hellenic harmony
mythical oxen yoked together.

Sun's rays power chlorophyll leaves
full moon's magic
powers reefs' polyps
to puff bubbles of life upward.

Moon's beauty, Sun's heat
two precious companions
to light our sphere.

Time to Smile

Argy-bargy

Plagiarism! said the Prof, it's a crime!
Your great idea, it's really mine!
I thought of it first, said the Fellow
I don't think you have a right to bellow!
Red-faced, they became quite heated
is that the way knowledge should be treated?
Threats were heard to take it to court
costing plenty, but ideas cannot be bought.
Argy-bargy continued loud and long
neither could tell right from wrong.
Then, lost for words – silence reigned
quiet breaths were heard, quite restrained.
I say, said the Prof, we could collaborate.
I'll drink to that, said the Fellow, let's celebrate.
Win at all costs, the game is lost.
Win-win, a victory without any cost.

Argy-bargy: argie is a Scottish dialect word meaning argue.

T-Bone

T-bone, quite a mouthful
funny bone, too painful.
Ham bone, not much for a troop
only enough for a pot of soup.

Walk into my physio's room
skeleton hangs from a boom.
Cracked bone, density low
calcium tabs hard to swallow.

Two cars crash, one T-boned
OUCH, side air bags explode.
Ambulance siren past many homes
hospital X-ray outlines her bones.

Pick up the dog and bone
(clever rhyming for telephone).
He never should have sent that text
take care any of us could be next.

The dam is bone dry, over there behind the shed
crazy cracks weave across its bed.
Cattle drink from windmill trough
how many T-bones is enough?

Brain Games

I think that it's just fantastic
to know the brain is like plastic
so, if I learn Hindustani
you might say I'm very brainy.

And how good for all the folk
unfortunate to have a stroke
they can work out in the gym
then punch the air with hand and limb.

For me, to stride aerobically
breathing air delightfully
how much more I will remember
from January until December.

Mathematics acrostic

Mathematicians solve equations on whiteboards
Albert Einstein's energy formula started the atomic age
Tangled metal monuments remaining at Maralinga.
Hundreds, thousands, millions of us made into statistics
Everyone's life measured and massaged
Multiplying makes us stronger, dividing makes us weaker.
Alan Turing's genius fathered the computer
Terabytes cruise along digital highways
Integers waited patiently until the zero was born
Calculations sent *Voyager 2* on course to Saturn
Scaling the heights – mathematicians are leading the way.

Belly Laugh

I like a good belly laugh
the Saturday movie's cream-pie fight
long ago, better by half
relaxed any muscles held far too tight.

Some jokes fly right over my head
far better those which make simple fun
of leaders who walk with serious tread
a palpable hit with a tasty cream bun.

Slapstick humour brings a great guffaw
has the audience falling about
everyone gives voice to a loud haw-haw
good for the health without any doubt.

Bully Boy

Beefy bully boy
bounced ball belligerently.
Daring Dan
decamped defiantly
returned with roaring water jet
brazenly blasted bully boy.
Bravo!

Winston's Words of Wisdom

from a candid canine

We dogs have clever looks
and no, we haven't learnt from books.
In misty time, to sounds of didgeridoo
we prowled campsites, found bones to chew.

We prick up our ears and wag our tails
It's a trick we've learnt, it never fails.
We come in all shapes and sizes
Labradoodles win dog show prizes.

Some of us herd sheep into races
others help in criminal chases.
When we go to obedience classes
we hope our owners receive their passes.

We have such good eyes and ears
help the blind cross roads without any fears.
We think we are very clever
no reason why we won't go on for ever and ever.

Previously Published

'Courage', 'Evacuate' and Listen Long' in *tamba*

The following poems in Ginninderra Press anthologies:
'Mawson's Hut' in *Wild* (2018)
'Fame' in *Mountain Secrets* (2019)
'Defiance 'in *I Protest! Poems of Dissent* (2020)
'Upward Stride' in *Milestones* (2021)

'Lyndoch', 'Sunday Afternoon' and' Pandemic Haiku' in the anthology *Plague Invasion* (editor, Carolyn Cordon)
'My Australia' in *The Bunyip*
'Rolling Money' in *The Senior*

Other publications by Geoff Graetz
Magical Sputnik (Ginninderra Press, 2014)
Music of our Sphere (chapbook, Ginninderra Press, 2018)

About the Author

During his more than thirty years serving as a Methodist and Uniting Church minister, Geoff Graetz enjoyed reading poetry. After attending a writing course in 2009, he began writing poetry and short stories. He has been a member of the Chapter and Verse writing group in Gawler, South Australia, for a number of years. His book of poems *Magical Sputnik* was published in 2014, followed by his chapbook *Music of Our Sphere* in 2018. His poems have been published in the journals *Positive Words, Write Angle* and *tamba* as well as in several anthologies published by Ginninderra Press. In 2017, he won first prize in the Gawler Public Library short story competition. He has contributed articles to the Gawler History website, to *Stories from the Significant Women of Gawler,* project edited by Elizabeth Mansutti (2010) and the anthology *Winged Pods* (Adelaide Plains Poets 2016).

www.ingramcontent.com/pod-product-compliance
Lightning Source LLC
Chambersburg PA
CBHW070331120526
44590CB00017B/2848